SERVING

A Server's Handbook

WITH COMPLINE

by

Denis E. Taylor, M.A.

*Lately Dean of Brisbane; former Director
of the General Board of Religious Education
of the Church of England in Australia,
Youth and Education Secretary of the
British Council of Churches*

REP

CONTENTS

THE SERVER

The server at the altar is highly privileged He ministers in the holy place, the Sanctuary of God's house, with holy things. Be he boy or man, he is in direct descent from the child Samuel who 'ministered unto the Lord before Eli the priest'.

The work is conspicuous. The server cannot be unnoticed. How vital that his performance of his duties be perfect, unobtrusive, dignified; and that his serving be an outward expression of his inward reverence for the things of God and of the worship he delights to offer to his Heavenly Father.

The server will be seen as regularly in the pew as he is in the sanctuary. The young man who comes to Church only when he is on duty should not be serving at all. Serving is an expression of the will to grow in grace and Christian living. It is not piety put on with the cassock and going no deeper.

The server will be regular and faithful in his own private prayers, in adoration and thanksgiving, in self-examination, confession, and intercession; he will read the Bible carefully; and he will rejoice to serve our Lord outside the walls of the church by helping his fellow men just as much as he delights to serve him in the sanctuary.

WHY WE DO THINGS DIFFERENTLY

Servers ask, Why does that church down the road use vestments at the Holy Communion? In ours the vicar wears a plain surplice with a stole.

'*That one has two*'

And down the road they genuflect and bow; we never do. Yet we are both the Church of England. It is very puzzling. Is one right and the other wrong?

On what principles are questions like these to be decided?

Servers in particular should have some understanding of these things. They should know the meaning of the ceremonial to which they are accustomed—exactly why they do this or that. They should also understand what is done in other parishes, because probably it is just as traditional and usual as what is done in their own. And they should understand why parishes thus do things differently—why one Anglican church uses or does not use this or that ceremony; why people bow in one church, but not in another; why this church has no candles on the altar, that one has two, whilst its neighbour has six—or even more. How can people approve or otherwise, like or dislike, or pass any intelligent judgement on practices about which they know neither the meaning nor the history?

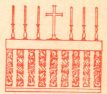

'*Its neighbour has six—or even more*'

Briefly, the ceremonial used in a church depends upon the 'tradition' of the parish. This also influences the ornaments of the sanctuary.

There are two main traditions in the Church of England, the Evangelical and the Catholic; but these two terms are not mutually exclusive. Each merges into the other. There are hundreds if not thousands of parishes (and the number is growing) which are half-way between. In them all the same Faith is taught, though one tradition may lay greater emphasis than another on particular aspects.

The *Evangelical* tradition (sometimes called *Low Church*) has roots which go back through Puritan times to the Reformation, and to the movements which led up to it. Thus the outlook of the Evangelical tradition is coloured by the Reformation protest against false teaching, superstition, and over-elaborate and largely meaningless ceremonial. With these Protestant sympathies the Evangelical tradition cherishes simplicity, and stresses everything gained at the Reformation, at the same time asserting its continuity and Catholic descent.

In most parishes of this tradition neither cross nor candle used to be found on the altar—'Holy Table' was the title preferred —but in recent years there has been some change in this. Outward signs of reverence, such as acknowledging the altar by a bow, remain unusual; and genuflecting would be regarded with distaste as verging on exhibitionism. There is suspicion of old practices now restored, lest these undermine the purity and simplicity of worship gained through centuries of struggle.

'*A plain surplice with stole*'

The emphasis in the Evangelical tradition is on an inward reverence of the spirit, not to be expressed in ornaments or outward actions such as bowing or making the sign of the Cross, lest these become a substitute for true devotion.

The *Catholic* tradition, on the other hand, believes that much that was good, as well as much that was bad, was

5

thrown overboard at the Reformation. This tradition stresses the continuity of the Church of England with the One, Holy, Catholic Church of the Apostles, the Creeds, and the Early Fathers. It values the rich inheritance of teaching and practice, of rite and ceremony, from those centuries before the Reformation when the Church in Europe was still one, though separated since 1054 from the Eastern Orthodox Churches. All most worth preserving in worship, teaching and ceremony, agreeable to Scripture, the Catholic would use again today.

'*Eucharistic vestments*'

Thus, in the Catholic tradition in the Church of England, the ancient Eucharistic vestments, cross, candles, bow and genuflexion, are used again, more because they increase the dignity, solemnity and beauty of worship than for any difference in teaching they may express. It is believed these outward acts and ornaments stimulate inward devotion.

HOW THESE OVERLAP

But the Church of England is one. In these two great traditions within her life, the *Evangelical* and the *Catholic*, different emphases in teaching and different expressions of worship are found; but the Church is essentially one. The two traditions overlap and merge into one another. It would be impossible to say where one ended and the other began. Some prefer Evangelical or Low Church simplicity and restraint in the externals of worship. Others find it bare and cold. Some think Catholic or High Church ways and ceremonial more helpful. Others are offended by it. Most seem to prefer the best of both traditions blended. We all have different tastes and temperaments, and what irritates one seems right to another.

The method of serving, therefore, depends largely upon the tradition of the particular parish. If it is in the extreme Evangelical tradition no one will bow towards the Holy Table, there will be no candles, no vestments, and no cross—and probably no servers either. But there will be the same reverence expressed in an inward, invisible way. At the opposite extreme, some churches in the Catholic tradition will use all these outward acts and ornaments, will certainly genuflect, and may even use incense too; and there will be many servers. The same reverence is being expressed in outward and visible ways. The more extreme churches in this tradition used to be called Anglo-Catholic, though that term is not heard so much today.

THE CHURCH OF ENGLAND IS ONE

The great mass of Anglican churches which belong to neither extreme use varying degrees of these ceremonies and ornaments. An increasing number today believe that the ancient Eucharistic vestments, genuflexion, bow, cross and candles create an atmosphere of worship and devotion and that they help considerably in kindling reverence, awe, and love.

Knowledge is essential. Because we are not used to something in our way of worship does not make it wrong; nor is there any guarantee that what we are used to and therefore like, is right or even the best way for others. (Toleration is necessary. Experience and the endeavour to understand the outlook of others brings sympathy and dispels prejudice.) The all-important fact is that the Church of England is one; and, because she goes back in unbroken continuity of worship, ministry and sacrament to the Church of our Lord and his Apostles, possesses an inheritance of unsurpassed wealth and diversity.

TO HEAL DIVISION

Today the devastating weakness that springs from the divisions of Christendom is recognised as never before.

7

The Church cannot command the respect of the world as long as Christians fail to agree. The splintering of the Body of Christ into Roman, Orthodox and Anglican; into Baptist, Presbyterian, and Congregationalist, Methodist and Quaker, and many other denominations and sects, is recognised as a grievous sin because it weakens the life and witness of the Church in the world. Jesus founded his Church to be one.

It is useless to bewail division and disunity unless we start at home inside the Anglican Communion, and get to know and understand those ways of worship different from our own but none the less traditional within the Church of England. We may still not like them, even when we have more knowledge and experience! The important thing is to be able to appreciate what they stand for and express. This can help the cause of unity.

ALTAR. Altar, font, Bible, with lectern and pulpit, are the essentials in a church for the observance of the two Gospel Sacraments and for the ministry of the Word, all commanded by our Lord. The altar is where the Holy Communion is celebrated. It is the most significant furnishing of the sanctuary. The whole architecture of the church is designed to draw the eye towards it. It may be made of wood or stone. It is sometimes known as the Holy Table, and is so called in the Book of Common Prayer. The top is often marked with five crosses representing the wounds of Christ. In many churches it is customary to turn towards the altar when passing in front and bow the head slightly—an acknowledgment that this is God's house and the altar speaks to us of his presence.

ALTAR CLOTH or Fair Linen. Made of white linen, the same breadth as the altar, it stretches its whole length and almost to the ground on either side. Often embroidered.

ALTAR COVER or dust cloth. White or coloured. Is placed over the Fair Linen when the altar is not being used.

ALTAR CROSS. The official sign of the Christian religion is usually found on the altar, the place of honour. The empty cross speaks of the Resurrection of Jesus, whom death could not hold. The crucifix proclaims the Incarnate God who offered himself as the 'one, full, perfect and sufficient sacrifice' for mankind. This, the main ornament of the sanctuary, is occasionally omitted if cross or crucifix occupies a prominent place in the carving of the reredos or if there is a Rood Screen. (Rood = Cross).

ALTAR FRONTAL. Cloth of rich material, often embroidered, covering the front of the altar. Usually there is a frontal of each liturgical colour (see page 16). Frontals not in use should be kept in a frontals case designed for them to hang unfolded.

AUMBRY. Small safe or cupboard in north wall of sanctuary in which consecrated Bread and Wine are kept for the Communion of the Sick. When the Sacrament is thus 'reserved' a white light may burn beside the aumbry.

BISHOP'S CHAIR. A chair for the Bishop always stands in the sanctuary on the north side.

BOWING. Is a sign of reverence and humility, enjoined in Scripture and commended in Canon Law. Custom varies greatly from church to church. To bow the head when passing in front of the altar and approaching and leaving the altar rails when receiving Holy Communion would seem to be the most usual practice (except in those churches which reject bowing altogether). In other churches servers bow when passing the altar, and when the name of Jesus is spoken; but from the Prayer of Consecration until the consecrated Bread and Wine of the Sacrament have been consumed they genuflect in recognition of the Real Presence (see Section *Serving Principles and Practices* page 23). In the Sarum Use the profound bow (i.e. from the waist) was practised, not genuflexion.

This is a subject to be discussed with your parish priest.

CANDLES. Some churches have no candles on the altar, others many. Two was the ancient Sarum Use, the most widespread in England. Some churches follow 'Western' or European practice and have six (or more) to add dignity to the altar. Candles remind us of Christ who is the 'Light to lighten the Gentiles' and the 'glory of his people'. Servers called 'taperers' may carry candles in a Gospel procession at the Eucharist when the Gospel is sung or said from the chancel step. This way of proclaiming the Gospel is designed to focus attention and pay honour to our Lord's own words and acts.

CHALICE. See page 27.

CREDENCE or Credence Table. A table or shelf on the

south of the sanctuary where the Bread Box, Wine and Water Cruets, Lavabo and Alms Dish stand at the Holy Communion.

DORSAL or Dossal. Curtains of rich material forming a background to the altar where there is no reredos. Curtains at the north and south ends of the altar are called 'riddels'. These may be supported by **riddel posts** sometimes surmounted by candles. An altar thus furnished with curtains is often called an **English Altar.**

FOOTPACE. The altar is usually raised some steps above the level of the sanctuary. The step or level on which the altar stands is called the **footpace.** The floor of the sanctuary, as distinct from the altar steps and footpace, is called the **pavement.**

GENUFLECTING. Means bowing the knee. In many churches the practice is to bow when passing the altar, but when the Bread and Wine have been consecrated to genuflect, go on one knee, acknowledging the **Real Presence** of our Lord (see *Principles and Practices* page 23).

INCENSE. The smoke of burning incense is symbolical of the prayers of the faithful ascending to God. It was used in the Temple services in Jerusalem and greatly favoured in the early Church. It is made of aromatic gums from certain trees. Charcoal is burned in a **censer** or **thurible** and kept alight by the draught of swinging. Incense taken from the 'boat' (usually carried by the youngest, smallest server) is sprinkled on the glowing charcoal by the officiating priest. The server bearing the incense is called the 'thurifer'. There is much prejudice against incense as a Roman custom, but its use has always been much wider than any one Christian communion.

PASCHAL CANDLE. A very large candle set up in some churches on Easter Eve. It is symbolical of the pillar of fire which guided the Israelites, and of the Light of the

Resurrection and Presence of Christ during the Forty Days before his Ascension. It is first lit during the ancient ceremonies of Easter Eve and thence until Ascension Day.

PAVEMENT. See Footpace above.

PISCINA. Shallow stone sink, often surmounted by canopy, in south wall of sanctuary, with drain leading direct into the earth. Used for the ablutions at Holy Communion so that these may not go into an ordinary drain. (Usually only found in old churches.)

RAILS (Altar). Protect the altar and divide the sanctuary from the chancel. Communicants kneel at the altar rails to receive Holy Communion.

REREDOS (Pronounced *rear-ee-doss*). Usually a carved structure, sometimes of great magnificence, rising behind the altar to help draw all eyes to the altar. Instead, there may be an altar piece called a triptych, a painting consisting of a central panel with hinged panels on either side which can be closed during Lent.

RIDDELS. See Dorsal above.

SANCTUARY LAMPS. One, three, or seven, hang in some churches before the main altar. Symbolic of the Godhead, the Holy Trinity, or the Seven Gifts of the Holy Spirit respectively. Should be fed with pure oil.

SANCTUS BELL. A gong or bell used in some churches and which stands on the south side of the sanctuary on the lowest step of the altar. Is sounded at the Sanctus, and three times at the consecration of both Bread and Wine. Announces the most solemn part of the Eucharist. May also be thought of as a welcome to him 'that cometh in the Name of the Lord'. It was valuable in the days when Mass was said in Latin and the people could not follow. A Sanctus Bell or Sacring, rung in some

A.—Altar Cross
B.—Dorsal Curtain
C.—Candlestick
D.—Burse
E.—Veil covering chalice
F.—Prayer Book
G.—Corporal
H.—Superfrontal

I. —Fair linen
J. —Frontal
K.—Riddel Post
L. —Footpace
M.—Standard Candle
N.—Lavabo bowl
O.—Box of wafer bread
P. —Cruet
Q.—Credence table

churches in the belfry lets the sick, or any within earshot, know that our Lord's sacrifice is being pleaded and that the Church is praying for them.

SEDILIA. A bench or group of three seats on the south side of the sanctuary used by celebrant and servers (or deacon and sub-deacon) during the Eucharist. Sometimes built at three levels when the celebrant takes the highest. Otherwise he sits in the centre.

STANDARD CANDLES. Two tall standard candlesticks are often placed on the pavement of the sanctuary, and lit for a Sung Eucharist.

SUPERFRONTAL. Hangs down over the top of the altar frontal. May be of same material, or is often of lace (see illustration, page 13).

TRIPTYCH. See Reredos above.

VESTMENTS. See page 17 f. for the names and derivation of the Eucharistic vessels and vestments. Not worn in every church. Evangelical parishes prefer the simplicity of the surplice. When surplice is used by clergy at a sacrament a stole usually accompanies it. At the choir offices of Mattins and Evensong a scarf and hood are worn with the surplice.

A triptych

CHURCH SEASONS AND LITURGICAL COLOURS

The seasons of the Christian Year are marked in most churches by the distinctive liturgical colour in altar frontal, vestments, markers, pulpit fall, etc.

Servers should know the sequence of the Christian Year. In ordinary life people would be hopelessly muddled and lost if they did not know which month and which season followed which. In church life they will be just as lost if they do not know the order of the seasons of the Christian Year.

As a rule it is not the server's duty to change the altar frontal, markers in the Lectern Bible, etc.; but there are occasions when these are forgotten, and the server can come to the rescue when he is laying out the vestments!

Most churches use a Calendar of the Christian Year which gives the date of each holy day and also indicates the liturgical colour. Such calendars are essential because so many festivals and holy days move according to the date of Easter, or if they fall on a more important day. It can be complicated working it out. For example, the Annunciation, or Lady Day (25th March), must be transferred if it falls any time from Palm Sunday, through Holy Week, to the end of the octave of Easter, because the whole of Holy Week and Easter rank as more important days.

So it is necessary to use the Church Calendar. But, even so, servers should know thoroughly the Christian Year, and the liturgical colour of each holy day, as well as its meaning.

The main colours are:

WHITE (or CREAM or GOLD) —the richest and best. So used for the joyful festivals, excepting Whitsunday. Also for saints and other martyrs.

RED represents fire and blood. Whitsunday and commemoration of martyrs.

PURPLE (or VIOLET) —for penitence and preparation. So used in Lent, Advent, Ember Days, Rogation Days, Vigils (i.e. the day of preparation before great festivals).

GREEN —the ordinary colour of nature, reminding us of God's provision for our daily needs. So green is used for the ordinary or 'ferial' Sundays.

Here is a 'ready reference' guide:

WHITE
Christmas
Epiphany
Easter
Ascension
Trinity Sunday
Festivals of the Virgin Mary
Michaelmas
All Saints Day

PURPLE
Advent
Lent (Septuagesima to Sat. in Holy Week) Note: some churches have special Lenten and Passion-tide hangings
Ember Days
Rogation Days
Vigils

RED
Whitsunday
Martyrs

GREEN
All 'ferial' or ordinary Sundays

ROBES, VESSELS AND VESTMENTS

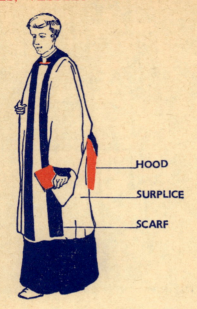

1. Priest vested in cassock and surplice, hood and scarf for the Choir Offices of Mattins and Evensong.

CASSOCK.—Long black gown once the daily dress of the clergy both indoors and outdoors. Also used by servers and choir.

SURPLICE.—Of white linen, reaching to the knee. Worn by clergy, choir and servers.

TIPPET. OF SCARF.—Black, worn usually with hood by clergy at Mattins and Evensong.

HOOD.—Was a medieval headdress. Today denotes University degree or Theological College. Each has its own distinctive colour.

17

SA—A*

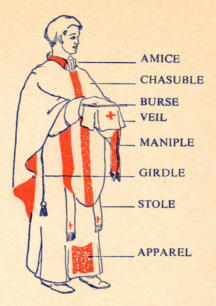

AMICE

CHASUBLE

BURSE

VEIL

MANIPLE

GIRDLE

STOLE

APPAREL

2. **Priest in Eucharistic Vestments and showing Burse and Veil.**

ALB,—Of white linen reaching to the ankles. Derived from the ancient Roman tunic. Used with girdle round the waist.

CHASUBLE.—Worn only when celebrating the Holy Communion. Is descended from the usual outdoor garments of Bible times.

AMICE.—Once a neckcloth, now a linen square to protect the neck of the chasuble.

STOLE.—Once a towel carried on the left shoulder to cleanse the sacred vessels. Worn by priest at the Sacraments.

ORPHREY.—The embroidered, usually cross-shaped strip on the chasuble. When not cross-shaped in front it is said to represent the pillar of Christ's scourging.

MANIPLE.—Originally a napkin. It is worn over the left arm by bishops, priests, and deacons at the Eucharist. It probably came into church life to cleanse the vessels after the stole had developed as above.

APPAREL.—Ornamented panels at the foot of the alb, front and back, and on amice. Not always used.

CROZIER,
OR
PASTORAL
STAFF—A
SHEPHERD'S
CROOK

HOOD

CHIMERE

SCARF

ROCHET

CASSOCK

3. Bishop in Rochet and Chimere, Hood and Scarf.

CHIMERE.—Long garment, black or scarlet, open in front, worn by Bishop over rochet.

ROCHET.—Long white garment like alb but used without girdle.

Most Church Vestments have come from the ordinary garb of a Roman citizen. Fashions altered, but the old styles were retained for use in Church.

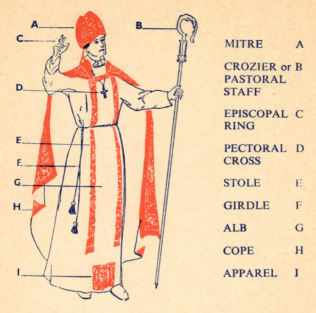

MITRE	A
CROZIER or PASTORAL STAFF	B
EPISCOPAL RING	C
PECTORAL CROSS	D
STOLE	E
GIRDLE	F
ALB	G
COPE	H
APPAREL	I

4. Bishop in Cope and Mitre.

COPE.—Once a long cloak, has become costly embroidered vestment worn by Bishops at Confirmations, Ordinations, etc. and by priests at Festivals.

MITRE.—Headdress of Bishop, tongue-shaped in remembrance of tongues of fire at Pentecost.

LAYING OUT VESTMENTS

In churches where vestments are used these are laid out before the Eucharist in order that the celebrant may vest in an orderly and recollected way, impossible if he has to burrow in drawers where several colours may be all mixed up or folded anyhow.

The vestments should be kept in a chest with shallow drawers or tray-drawers, three to four inches deep, each liturgical colour having a drawer to itself.

The picture seen here shows how the vestments are arranged on top of the vestments chest or on a special table for the celebrant to robe. They are put away in their special drawer afterwards laid out in the same way. On top of the chest or table there should be a spotless white cloth.

1. Lay the chasuble out flat, front downwards.

2. Lift back and front into two or three loose folds so that it does not hang over the front of the chest or table. It is now so arranged that the priest may simply pick up the back and drop it over his head.

3. On top of the chasuble place the stole folded to the shape of an H. This is done by putting the cross at the neck of the stole in the centre of the chasuble. About eight to ten inches to either side fold as shown above. Now only the front of the stole is seen, the reverse side being folded under. The whole stole makes the letter H.

4. On top of the stole place the maniple. It forms the letter I.

5. On top of both lay the girdle, doubled, or if it is a long one, fourfold, in the shape of an S.

These three items are now lying in the shape of the monogram of IHS.

The Greek way of writing JESUS is IHΣYΣ and the first three letters IHΣ were used as a Christian symbol in the Early Church. This was easily mistaken for the Latin IHS, and has come down to us in that form (see below).

Words to fit the letters (Jesus Hominum Salvator = Jesus the Saviour of Men; I Have Suffered, etc.) were wrongly added later.

6. Now lay the alb front downwards on top of the vestments, so arranged that the bottom of the back of the alb is to the top, in much the same way as the chasuble, so that it will easily slip over the celebrant's head.

7. The amice is spread out flat over everything else, the tapes straightened out to form a St. Andrew's cross.

The priest vests in the reverse order to the above, namely

Amice: Alb: Girdle: Maniple: Stole: Chasuble.

Laying out the vestments takes a long time to describe, but with practice it can easily be done in three minutes. And what a satisfaction and delight to have a tidy sacristy with spotless white linen cloths, the vestments properly laid out for the Eucharist, and the Chalice 'made' and standing in its proper place!

After the service, vestments should be put away in their shallow drawers arranged in the same way with the minimum of folds, care being taken to see that these folds are never twice running in quite the same place.

22

No Handbook can cover all variations of practice common in the Anglican Communion today. This book gives only those which are most used and have best authority.

What is known as the Liturgical Movement is having much influence at present in the Anglican, Roman and many other Communions. In its way it is a kind of 'Little Reformation'. It is seeking to rid the Eucharist of late and less helpful accretions and to restore its original purity and simplicity. Several of the points listed below under the heading 'At the Eucharist' are the result of the Liturgical Movement.

It is most important to remember that good serving shuns anything that savours of ostentation, exaggerated outward devotion, or fussiness. Restraint, dignity, and simplicity are the marks of good serving. The server, if possible, should just not be noticed.

Most of the practical points which follow spring from one or other of these basic principles.

General

MOVING. A server should walk at a normal pace—not so slowly as to appear studied, nor yet hurrying. All movements should be made with naturalness, deliberation, and dignity.

A server should never step sideways or backwards. This looks to the congregation like shuffling. To go even one yard to the left the server turns left, walks to the new position, then turns right again to face the altar. He makes these turns naturally—not as if on a parade ground.

A server should never 'cut the corner'. For example, to

reach the credence the straight route would involve crossing the lowest step of the altar. This would be incorrect. The server walks along the pavement until in line with the credence, then turns left and approaches it.

HANDS. When the server is walking, his hands should be held clasped in front, at waist level; or they may hang down clasped in front. It is unnatural and fussy to keep the fingers pointing out straight with tips together as if in prayer.

RESPONSES. Few servers seem to realise that to lead the congregation clearly and audibly in the Creed, the General Confession, the Responses, Amens, etc., is an important part of the server's office; quite as important as his other duties. When learning to serve, this side of the work should be practised and the level of voice necessary should be found. Too often, servers are inaudible.

At the Eucharist

THE PREPARATION—said by priest and server beforehand. Some think that this is better said in the vestry immediately before entering the sanctuary, on the principle that everything after the service commences should be shared by priest and people.

THE REAL PRESENCE. This phrase needs explanation. The Church of England, very wisely, has never officially defined what happens to the Bread and Wine of the Sacrament at the Prayer of Consecration in the Holy Communion. Anglican sympathies are all with Queen Elizabeth who, four hundred years ago, is credited with these words:

> *His was the Word that spake it.*
> *He took the Bread and brake it,*
> *And what His Word doth make it,*
> *I do believe and take it.*

We all know the word of Jesus at the Last Supper, 'This is my Body . . .' Many Christians believe that Christ, always present in his world and with his people, is even more intimately present when believers meet together to obey his command, 'Do this in remembrance of me', and to receive the gift that he appointed. We call this presence of our Lord when related to the Sacrament the Real Presence. Jesus comes to us. The Church does not attempt to define it more closely than that.

The Real Presence is acknowledged, when serving (in some churches) by a deeper reverence, called the 'profound bow', or by genuflexion. These are explained below.

For the same reason the server will never sit during the Communion of the People. He is in the King's presence.

Bow, Profound Bow, Genuflexion.
These are all much used today, though not in all churches. Servers should understand them.

THE ORDINARY BOW (head only) is used
(*a*) To acknowledge the altar.
(*b*) When the name of Jesus is spoken in hymn, scripture, etc.
(*c*) When an action in serving has been completed— instead of saying 'Thank You'.

THE PROFOUND BOW (from the waist and so that the hands if hanging straight down would just touch the knees), was customary in the ancient Sarum use, the most widespread in England. It is used
(*a*) at the *Incarnatus* in the Creed, and
(*b*) in reverence for the Real Presence. So the profound bow is used from the Consecration until after the Ablutions.

25

THE GENUFLEXION—dropping on the right knee with the back and head held straight—took the place of the profound bow in the later Middle Ages.

The purpose of this book is to explain, not to direct. Therefore, in the instructions for serving at the Eucharist, the term 'reverence' is used. This will be interpreted as meaning bow, profound bow, or genuflexion, according to the use of the parish at that point.

The server will follow the directions of his priest.

THE PRAYER OF OBLATION is said as a continuation of the Prayer of Consecration (page 43) in some churches, because this was its original position. This is noted in the text (page 44).

THE ABLUTIONS. The Prayer Book directs that these be taken after the Blessing, and it could be wished that this was the practice everywhere. In some churches, however, the Ablutions are taken immediately after the Communion of the People. This is noted in the text (page 48).

REMOVING ALTAR BOOK to south end. Whatever the practice regarding the Ablutions there is no practical object served (and it is therefore bad practice) to remove the Altar Book to the south (right) of the altar after the Communion, and similarly the veil to the left. The *Our Father*, the *Prayer of Oblation* (or its alternative the *Prayer of Thanksgiving*), the *Gloria in Excelsis*, and the *Blessing* are to be said in the centre; and the Altar Book should remain on the left where it has been since the Creed.*

THE LAST GOSPEL. (That appointed for Christmas Day.) Was formerly recited aloud or said privately after the Blessing. This is now usually omitted.

* See *A Directory of Ceremonial* (Alcuin Club).

26

SERVING AT HOLY COMMUNION

BEFORE THE SERVICE

PRELIMINARIES

1. *Put on cassock.* Surplice, cotta, or alb is not usually put on until preparatory work is completed.

2. *Go and kneel* in a quiet, unseen spot and say a prayer. Offer the work you are going to do to God and ask his blessing on it and on you.

3. *Uncover the altar* (while there are still few in church) folding the dust cover neatly and putting it in its appointed place.

IN THE VESTRY OR SACRISTY

1. *Prepare cruets,* filling with wine and fresh water.

2. *Fill bread box.* If wafer breads are used count them into tens or whatever number is customary.

3. *Prepare lavabo:* water in jug, clean towel, basin.

4. *'Make' the chalice,* as illustrated below:

    (*a*) Place folded purificator over chalice.

    (*b*) Put paten above purificator on chalice.

    (*c*) Put priest's wafer on paten.

    (*d*) Cover with pall.

    (*e*) Cover with silk veil of liturgical colour of the day.

    (*f*) Place corporal and fine linen veil in burse and place on chalice

5. *Lay out Vestments.* See page 21.

A.—BURSE

B.—BREAD

C.—PATEN

D.—PURIFICATOR

E.—CHALICE

F.—CORPORAL

1. *Take out cruets, bread box and lavabo,* and arrange on credence, cruet handles turned away from you. (Note: to minimise traffic in sanctuary, disturbing to worshippers, use a tray just large enough to hold these).

2. *Light candles.* Epistle side (south, right) first. Standard candles are lit only at a Sung Eucharist.

3. *See that the markers are in their right places* in the Altar Book. (Collect or collects for the day. Holy Communion.) But in many churches the Prayer Book is carried in by the server at the commencement.

4. *Carry in the chalice,* 'made' as above, only if it is a Sung Eucharist. Take corporal from the burse, spread exactly in the centre of the altar (the base of the altar cross often gives a good guide to centre) with the edge of the corporal exactly reaching the front of the altar but not hanging over. Having spread the corporal, the chalice covered by the veil is placed in the centre of the corporal (see page 13). The burse stands on the altar towards the left. At a said, or 'low', celebration the priest carries the chalice with him when he enters to commence the service.

5. *See that the servers' books are in position.* Place a hymn-book on altar for celebrant (at the back, right of centre).

Now put on surplice or cotta, pick up altar book if it is carried in, and all conversation should cease. Stand quietly waiting and remember God's presence.

which may be said by priest and server before the Holy Communion.

Priest: In the Name of the Father, and of the Son, and of the Holy Ghost.
Server: Amen.

Priest: I will go unto the Altar of God.
Server: Even unto the God of my joy and gladness.

Priest: Give sentence with me, O God, and defend my cause against the ungodly people: O deliver me from the deceitful and wicked man.
Server: For thou art the God of my strength, why hast thou put me from thee: and why go I so heavily, while the enemy oppresseth me?

Priest: O send out thy light and thy truth, that they may lead me: and bring me unto thy holy hill, and to thy dwelling.
Server: And that I may go unto the altar of God, even unto the God of my joy and gladness: and upon the harp will I give thanks unto thee, O God, my God.

Priest: Why art thou so heavy, O my soul: and why art thou so disquieted within me?
Server: O put thy trust in God: for I will yet give him thanks, which is the help of my countenance, and my God.

Priest: Glory be to the Father, and to the Son, and to the Holy Ghost;
Server: As it was in the beginning, is now and ever shall be, world without end. Amen.

Priest: I will go unto the altar of God.
Server: Even unto the God of my joy and gladness.

Priest: Our help is in the Name of the Lord;
Server: Who hath made heaven and earth.

Priest: I confess to God Almighty, the Father, the Son, and the Holy Ghost, before the whole company of heaven, and to you, my brother, that I have sinned exceedingly, in thought, word, and deed, through my fault, through my own fault, through my own most grievous fault; wherefore I pray God to have mercy upon me and you, my brother, to pray to the Lord our God for me.

Server: **Almighty God have mercy upon thee, forgive thee thy sins, and bring thee to everlasting life.**

Priest: Amen.

Server: **I confess to God Almighty, the Father, the Son, and the Holy Ghost, before the whole company of heaven, and to you, my father, that I have sinned exceedingly in thought, word, and deed, through my fault, through my own fault, through my own most grievous fault; wherefore I pray God to have mercy upon me, and you, my father, to pray to the Lord our God for me.**

Priest: Almighty God have mercy upon thee, forgive thee thy sins, and bring thee to everlasting life.

Server: **Amen.**

Priest: The Almighty and most merciful Lord grant us pardon, absolution, and remission of all our sins.

Server: **Amen.**

Priest: Wilt thou not turn again and quicken us, O Lord?

Server: **That thy people may rejoice in thee.**

Priest: O Lord, shew thy mercy upon us.
Server: **And grant us thy salvation.**

Priest: Lord, hear our prayer.
Server: **And let our cry come unto thee.**

Priest: The Lord be with you.
Server: **And with thy spirit.**

Priest: Let us pray.

The priest will now begin THE LORD'S PRAYER.

(A blue line in the margin marks the places where the server responds or has duties.)

Server precedes priest, goes sufficiently past entrance of sanctuary to let priest come to centre. Both make reverence. Server enters after priest, kneels on left (opposite side to Altar Book) unless Preparation is said, when server kneels on pavement a little left of centre allow celebrant to stand in centre.

After Preparation, server rises, goes to left side, stands, if an Introit hymn is being sung, then kneels.

THE INTRODUCTION

The priest says this prayer and the Amen by himself. (It was once said privately.)

OUR FATHER, ... Amen.

And he prays that we may love and worship God truly:

ALMIGHTY GOD, unto whom all hearts be open, all desires known, and from whom no secrets are hid; Cleanse the thoughts of our hearts by the inspiration of thy Holy Spirit, that we may perfectly love thee and worthily magnify thy holy name; through Christ our Lord.

Server: **Amen.**

Either

THE TEN COMMANDMENTS

Because all have sinned God's ancient Law is read and we ask His mercy.

Server leads people in the responses.

OUR DUTY TO GOD

GOD spake these words, and said:

I. I am the Lord thy God: Thou shalt have none other gods but me.

Server: Lord, have mercy upon us, and incline our hearts to keep this law.

(*repeated after each commandment*)

II. Thou shalt not make to thyself any graven image, nor the likeness of any thing that is in heaven above, or in the earth beneath or in the water under the earth. Thou shalt not bow down to them, nor worship them.

III. Thou shalt not take the name of the Lord thy God in vain.

IV. Remember that thou keep holy the Sabbath day. Six days shalt thou labour, and do all that thou hast to do; but the seventh day is the Sabbath of the Lord thy God.

OUR DUTY TO OUR NEIGHBOUR

V. Honour thy father and thy mother.

VI. Thou shalt do no murder.

VII. Thou shalt not commit adultery.

VIII. Thou shalt not steal.

IX. Thou shalt not bear false witness.

X. Thou shalt not covet.

Server: Lord, have mercy upon us and write all these Thy laws in our hearts, we beseech Thee.

Or   (1928)   Or

THE SUMMARY OF THE LAW

quoted by our Lord

OUR Lord Jesus Christ said: Hear O Israel, The Lord our God is one Lord: and thou shalt love the Lord thy God with all thy heart, and with all thy soul, and with all thy mind, and with all thy strength: This is the first commandment. And the second is like, namely this. Thou shalt love thy neighbour as thyself. There is none other commandment greater than these.

On these two commandments hang all the Law and the Prophets.

Server: Lord, have mercy upon us, and incline our hearts to keep this law.

THE KYRIES

addressed to the Three Persons of The Holy Trinity, are sung or said, as we draw near in humble penitence.

Lord, have mercy.
Christ have mercy.
Lord, have mercy.

Or, *in the ninefold form*

Priest: Lord, have mercy.
Server: Lord, have mercy.

Priest: Lord have mercy.
Server: Christ, have mercy.

Priest: Christ, have mercy.
Server: Christ, have mercy.

Priest: Lord, have mercy.
Server: Lord, have mercy.

Priest: Lord, have mercy.

Or, *in Greek*

Priest: Kyrie, eleison.
Server: Christe, eleison.
Priest: Kyrie, eleison.

Then the priest may say:

The Lord be with you:

Server: And with thy spirit.

Let us pray.

33

Here may be said the Prayer for the Queen, and then

THE COLLECT

or special prayer (or prayers) for the Sunday or Holy day
the server leading the people's Amens.

THE MINISTRY OF THE WORD

The server usually continues to kneel, but may stand if he
wishes, for

THE EPISTLE

The Apostles wrote letters to encourage and instruct the
early Christians. Their words—or other passages from
the Old or New Testament—still help us today and God
speaks to us through them.

On the words 'Here endeth the Epistle' the server(s) rises
quickly. Server on left removes Altar Book (always with
cushion or stand) to left (north) end of the altar, not
making any reverence as he crosses.
Goes to right side (always opposite side to Book) if serving alone. Stands facing Gospeller.

THE GOSPEL

When the Gospel is announced

Server: Glory be to thee, O Lord.

And at the conclusion

Server: Praise be to thee, O Christ.

The priest will now move the Altar Book towards the
middle, and returning to centre he begins the Creed

THE NICENE CREED

Priest: I BELIEVE IN ONE GOD

Server: the Father Almighty, Maker of heaven and earth, And of all things visible and invisible:

And in one Lord Jesus Christ, the only begotten Son of God, Begotten of his Father before all worlds, God of God, Light of Light, Very God of very God, Begotten, not made, Being of one substance with the Father, By whom all things were made: Who for us men, and for our salvation came down from heaven,

Priest and server may make reverence at this stupendous statement:

And was incarnate by the Holy Ghost of the Virgin Mary, And was made man,

And was crucified also for us under Pontius Pilate. He suffered and was buried, And the third day he rose again according to the Scriptures, And ascended into heaven, And sitteth on the right hand of the Father. And he shall come again with glory to judge both the quick and the dead: Whose kingdom shall have no end.

And I believe in the Holy Ghost, The Lord, The giver of life, Who proceedeth from the Father and the Son, Who with the Father and the Son together is worshipped and glorified, Who spake by the Prophets. And I believe one Catholick and Apostolick Church. I acknowledge one Baptism for the remission of sins. And I look for the Resurrection of the dead. And the Life of the world to come. Amen.

THE SERMON

When there is a sermon, towards end of Creed:
make reverence with celebrant. Go to sedilia. (If celebrant is also preacher he may take off chasuble.
At sedilia stand between him and congregation while he
does this. Lay chasuble on sedilia or altar.) Sit when
sermon has been announced.

THE OFFERTORY

Immediately after Creed or Sermon server(s) goes to
credence.

*The Offertory sentence from the Bible is said. A hymn may
be sung.*

Server A hands to celebrant
the ciborium (if used). Then
the bread box, with lid open.

Server B meanwhile has taken off
stoppers, takes cruets, handles towards celebrant, the wine in right
hand, and offers them. As priest
pours wine, transfer water to empty
right hand. When priest takes water transfer wine to
empty right hand. This has made the sign of the cross.

Server A meanwhile takes Alms
Dish, receives collection from
sidesmen, brings it to celebrant's right side. He offers
alms and places alms dish at
right end of altar.

Server B now ready with lavabo,
towel over left wrist, pours
water over celebrant's fingers.

Server A closes altar rail. Waits
at right for *B.*

A and *B* together move to centre, make reverence, go to their places and kneel.

Note : *If there is only one server he does all these duties in the order set out. He should uncork the cruets before he offers the Bread Box.*

THE PRAYER FOR THE CHURCH

We pray for the whole Church, in this world and the next. The priest bids:

Let us pray for the whole state of Christ's Church militant here in earth.

And he may ask particular intercessions and thanksgivings to be included.

ALMIGHTY and everliving God, who by thy holy Apostle hast taught us to make prayers, and supplications, and to give thanks, for all men :

Ask God to accept our money and our offering of ourselves

We humbly beseech thee most mercifully to accept our alms and oblations, and to receive these our prayers, which we offer unto thy Divine Majesty;

Pray that Church and people may be Christlike

beseeching thee to inspire continually the universal Church with the spirit of truth, unity, and concord; And grant that all they that do confess thy holy name may agree in the truth of thy holy Word, and live in unity, and godly love.

Pray for the Queen and Commonwealth

We beseech thee also to save and defend all Christian Kings, Princes and Governors; and specially thy Servant ELIZABETH our Queen; that under her we may be godly and quietly governed; And grant unto her whole Council, and to all that are put in authority under her, that they may truly and indifferently minister justice, to the punishment of wickedness and vice, and to the maintenance of thy true religion, and virtue.

Pray for the clergy, especially your own

Give grace, O heavenly Father, to all Bishops and Curates, that they may both by their life and doctrine set forth thy true and lively Word, and rightly and duly administer thy holy Sacraments:

Pray for all, not least for your own parish

And to all thy people give thy heavenly grace; and specially to this congregation here present; that with meek heart and due reverence, they may hear, and receive thy holy Word; truly serving thee in holiness and righteousness all the days of their life.

Pray for all in suffering

And we most humbly beseech thee of thy goodness, O Lord, to comfort and succour all them, who in this transitory life are in trouble, sorrow, need, sickness, or any other adversity.

Thank God for all who have lived faithfully and well

And we also bless thy holy name for all thy servants departed this life in thy faith and fear; beseeching thee to give us grace so to follow their good examples, that with them we may be partakers of thy heavenly kingdom: Grant this, O Father, for Jesus Christ's sake, our only Mediator and Advocate.

Server: **Amen.**

THE PREPARATION FOR COMMUNION
THE INVITATION

Think of the sacred moment when we shall receive the Body and Blood of the Lord Jesus in the Holy Communion. We are invited to draw near with faith. First we must confess our sins, especially those which our preparation made clear to us.

The Priest turns to the people, and says:

YE that do truly and earnestly repent you of your sins, and are in love and charity with your neighbours, and intend to lead a new life, following the commandments of God, and walking from henceforth in his holy ways: Draw near with faith, and take this Holy Sacrament to your comfort; and make your humble confession to Almighty God, meekly kneeling upon your knees.

THE CONFESSION

Kneeling, the server leads the Confession in a voice strong enough for all to hear and keep together:

ALMIGHTY GOD, Father of our Lord Jesus Christ, Maker of all things, Judge of all men; We acknowledge and bewail our manifold sins and wickedness, Which we, from time to time, most grievously have committed, By thought, word, and deed, Against thy divine Majesty, Provoking most justly thy wrath and indignation against us. We do earnestly repent, And are heartily sorry for these our misdoings; The remembrance of them is grievous unto us; The burden of them is intolerable. Have mercy upon us, Have mercy upon us, most merciful Father; For thy Son our Lord Jesus Christ's sake, Forgive us all that is past; and grant that we may ever hereafter Serve and please thee In newness of life, To the honour and glory of thy Name; Through Jesus Christ our Lord. Amen.

THE ABSOLUTION

God's answer of forgiveness to those who are really trying.

ALMIGHTY God, our heavenly Father, who of his great mercy hath promised forgiveness of sins to all them that with hearty repentance and true faith turn unto him: Have mercy upon you; pardon and deliver you from all your sins; confirm and strengthen you in all goodness; and bring you to everlasting life; through Jesus Christ our Lord.

Server: **Amen.**

THE COMFORTABLE WORDS
(OR WORDS OF ENCOURAGEMENT)

Words which have rejoiced Christians in all ages and given them new courage and hope:

Hear what comfortable words our Saviour Christ saith unto all that truly turn to him.

COME unto me all that travail and are heavy laden, and I will refresh you.

So God loved the world, that he gave his only-begotten Son, to the end that all that believe in him should not perish, but have everlasting life.

Hear also what St. Paul saith:

This is a true saying, and worthy of all men to be received, That Christ Jesus came into the world to save sinners.

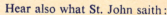

Hear also what St. John saith:

If any man sin, we have an Advocate with the Father, Jesus Christ the righteous; and he is the propitiation for our sins.

The Prayer of Humble Access, p. 42, may be said here. (1928)

40

THE CONSECRATION

Our Lord's mighty act of redemption is set forth. Jesus himself draws near to us and we to him.

First, we worship and thank God with all the members of his Family the Church, on earth and in paradise, and with the Holy Angels.

Priest: The Lord be with you;

Server: And with thy spirit.

Priest: Lift up your hearts;

Server: We lift them up unto the Lord.

Priest: Let us give thanks unto our Lord God.

Server: It is meet and right so to do.

It is very meet, right, and our bounden duty, that we should at all times and in all places, give thanks unto thee, O Lord, Holy Father, Almighty, Everlasting God.

At the great Festivals and on Saints' Days, Proper Prefaces—sentences about that holy day—are added here.

Therefore with Angels and Archangels and with all the company of heaven, we laud and magnify thy glorious Name; evermore praising thee, and saying,

HOLY, HOLY, HOLY

Priest and Server: Holy, holy, holy, Lord God of hosts, heaven and earth are full of thy glory; Glory be to thee, O Lord, most High. Amen.

Jesus promised 'I will not leave you strengthless. I will come to you.' Because Jesus comes to us now we welcome him as the people in Jerusalem did:

Priest and Server: Blessed is he that cometh in the Name of the Lord. Hosanna in the highest.

(1928)

THE PRAYER OF HUMBLE ACCESS

Our Lord is Very God of Very God. We are sinners. We must come into his Presence humbly and penitently.

WE do not presume to come to this thy Table, O merciful Lord, trusting in our own righteousness, but in thy manifold and great mercies. We are not worthy so much as to gather up the crumbs under thy Table. But thou art the same Lord, whose property is always to have mercy; Grant us therefore, gracious Lord, so to eat the Flesh of thy dear Son Jesus Christ, and to drink his Blood, that our sinful bodies may be made clean by his Body, and our souls washed through his most precious Blood, and that we may evermore dwell in him, and he in us.

| *Server:* Amen.

42

We draw near. 'Where two or three are gathered in My Name, there am I.' The living Christ is in our midst. We bow our heads in wonder and love.

If desired, the server may sound gong or bell to call the people to recollection.

ALMIGHTY God, our heavenly Father, who of thy tender mercy didst give thine only Son Jesus Christ to suffer death upon the Cross for our redemption; who made there (by his one oblation of himself once offered) a full, perfect, and sufficient sacrifice, oblation, and satisfaction, for the sins of the whole world; and did institute, and in his holy Gospel command us to continue, a perpetual memory of that his precious death, until his coming again;

Hear us, O merciful Father, we most humbly beseech thee; and grant that we receiving these thy creatures of bread and wine, according to thy Son our Saviour Jesus Christ's holy institution, in remembrance of his death and passion, may be partakers of his most blessed Body and Blood:

(*Now the Celebrant repeats our Lord's actions at the Last Supper. He takes bread—he offers our lives that Christ may lift us up with his Sacrifice. He breaks the bread. Christ's body was broken on the cross—the reign of God in the lives of men can only come through self-sacrifice. He lays his hands on the bread and on the wine that these offerings, and all they represent, may be accepted by God and made holy.*)

Who, in the same night that he was betrayed, took bread; and, when he had given thanks, he brake it, and gave it to his disciples, saying, TAKE, EAT, THIS IS MY BODY WHICH IS GIVEN FOR YOU: DO THIS IN REMEMBRANCE OF ME.

Here the server may sound Sanctus Bell.

Likewise after supper he took the Cup; and, when he had given thanks, he gave it to them, saying, DRINK YE ALL OF THIS; FOR THIS IS MY BLOOD OF THE NEW TESTAMENT, WHICH IS SHED FOR YOU AND FOR MANY FOR THE REMISSION OF SINS: DO THIS, AS OFT AS YE SHALL DRINK IT, IN REMEMBRANCE OF ME.

Server: **Amen.**

Here server may sound Sanctus Bell.

In some churches the Prayer of Oblation or Offering is added at this point to the Prayer of Consecration, this being its ancient position.

Turn to page 48. Prayer of Oblation.

The OUR FATHER, *in which the server joins, will probably follow. Then*

Priest: The peace of God be alway with you.

Server: And with thy spirit.　　　　　　　(1928)

THE COMMUNION

Jesus is with us. We are in his Presence. In the holy silence, kneeling before him, we present before God the sacrifice of Jesus for us on the Cross.

Have all these thoughts and prayers in your heart as you plead:

Priest and Server:

O Lamb of God, that takest away the sin of the world, have mercy upon us. (Repeat.)

O Lamb of God, that takest away the sin of the world, grant us thy peace.

Now the priest will make his own Communion.

44

As you kneel think of **Jesus on the Cross**. In your heart be saying,

Jesu, my Lord, I thee adore;
O make me love thee more and more.

Pray for the Priest.

The server has the privilege of receiving the Sacrament first, before all the people. If possible remain kneeling in the same place.

The Priest gives you

The Bread . . . of which Jesus said 'THIS IS MY BODY. . . .'

The Wine . . . of which Jesus said 'THIS IS MY BLOOD. . . .'

Servers rise together.

Offer reverence.

Move to either end of the altar.

Stand during the Communion of the people, facing partly towards the altar, partly east.

SERVER'S PRAYERS DURING THE COMMUNION OF THE PEOPLE

Remember our Lord is here. We are in the King's Presence. Do not waste one moment of this precious time.

Plead in this solemn moment the perfect life of Jesus and his dying for us. Read these words slowly and thoughtfully,

And now, O Father, mindful of the love
    That bought us, once for all, on Calvary's tree,
And having with us Him that pleads above,
    We here present, we here spread forth to Thee
That only offering perfect in Thine eyes,
The one true, pure, immortal sacrifice.

Only because Jesus died on our behalf dare we offer ourselves and ask God to accept us. Read very slowly:

Look, Father, look on His anointed face
    And only look on us as found in Him;
Look not on our misusings of Thy Grace,
    Our prayer so languid and our faith so dim.
For lo, between our sins and their reward
We set the Passion of Thy Son, our Lord.

But we are not here chiefly to pray for ourselves but to be about our Father's business, not least his work of Intercession:

Think about the matters or people the priest spoke of when he asked us to pray 'for the whole state of Christ's Church'. Hold these up to God and say silently: Lord, hear our prayer, and let our cry come unto Thee.

Make the fullest use of these precious moments of silent prayer in the Presence of Jesus.

Especially :-

From your Preparation bring to Jesus now

Your special thanksgivings ....

....

Your special confessions ....

....

Your special petitions ....

....

Pray for your family and home.

It helps to note these on a slip of paper.

The way of Jesus means surrender of self, the willingness to give ourselves completely, that God may take and use our wills surrendered to him.

As last communicant leaves the altar rails

Return to centre of pavement.
Make reverence.
Kneel in usual place. (But see Note below.)

All our intercessions and thanksgivings are summed up now in Christ's own prayer:

Priest and Server: OUR FATHER, ... for ever and ever. Amen.

THE THANKSGIVING

Either

THE PRAYER OF OFFERING (OBLATION)

We offer ourselves, our whole lives, to God through Jesus Christ.

O LORD and heavenly Father, we thy humble servants entirely desire thy fatherly goodness mercifully to accept this our sacrifice of praise and thanksgiving; most humbly beseeching thee to grant, that by the merits and death of thy Son Jesus Christ, and through faith in his blood, we and all thy whole Church may obtain remission of our sins, and all other benefits of his passion.

AND HERE WE OFFER AND PRESENT UNTO THEE, O LORD, OURSELVES, OUR SOULS AND BODIES,

to be a reasonable, holy and lively sacrifice unto thee; humbly beseeching thee, that all we, who are partakers of this Holy Communion, may be fulfilled with thy grace and heavenly benediction.

And although we be unworthy, through our manifold sins, to offer unto thee any sacrifice, yet we beseech thee to

---

Note: *In some churches the Ablutions are taken at this point. Turn to page 51 ABLUTIONS.*

48

accept this our bounden duty and service; not weighing our merits, but pardoning our offences, through Jesus Christ our Lord; by whom and with whom, in the unity of the Holy Ghost, all honour and glory be unto thee, O Father Almighty, world without end.

Server: **Amen.**

Or

THE PRAYER OF THANKSGIVING

Thank God for the precious privilege of Communion.

ALMIGHTY and everliving God, we most heartily thank thee, for that thou dost vouchsafe to feed us, who have duly received these holy mysteries, with the spiritual food of the most precious Body and Blood of thy Son our Saviour Jesus Christ;

Thank God for membership in his Family, the Church.

AND dost assure us thereby of thy favour and goodness towards us;
And that we are very members incorporate in the mystical body of thy Son, which is the blessed company of all faithful people; and are also heirs through hope of thy everlasting kingdom, by the merits of the most precious death and passion of thy dear Son.

Pray for the grace of perseverance.

AND we most humbly beseech thee, O heavenly Father, so to assist us with thy grace, that we may continue in that holy fellowship, and do all such good works as thou hast prepared for us to walk in; through Jesus Christ our Lord, to whom, with thee and the Holy Ghost, be all honour and glory, world without end.

Server: **Amen.**

THE GLORIA IN EXCELSIS

The Last Supper ended with a hymn as our Lord set out for the Garden of Gethsemane. The Lord's Own Service ends with one of the most ancient hymns of Christendom —a pæan of praise and prayer.

GLORY BE TO GOD ON HIGH, and in earth peace, good will towards men. We praise thee, we bless thee, we worship thee, we glorify thee, we give thanks to thee for thy great glory, O Lord God, heavenly King, God the Father Almighty.

O Lord, the only-begotten Son Jesu Christ; O Lord God, Lamb of God, Son of the Father, that takest away the sins of the world, have mercy upon us.

Thou that takest away the sins of the world, have mercy upon us. Thou that takest away the sins of the world, receive our prayer. Thou that sittest at the right hand of God the Father, have mercy upon us.

For thou only art holy; thou only art the Lord; thou only, O Christ, with the Holy Ghost, art most high in the glory of God the Father. **Amen.**

THE BLESSING

We are sent forth with the Blessing of God on our lives and his wonder and joy in our hearts. We rejoice specially that we are never alone and on our own; but are members one of another and of God's Family the Church, and that he is with us always.

THE PEACE of God, which passeth all understanding, keep your hearts and minds in the knowledge and love of God, and of his Son Jesus Christ our Lord:

And the blessing of God Almighty, the Father, the Son, and the Holy Ghost, be amongst you and remain with you always.

Server: **Amen.**

Here may follow a hymn.

THE ABLUTIONS*

Immediately after the Blessing,
  Server(s) rise.
  Offer reverence.
  Go to credence.
Server B uncorks and takes up by the handles both cruets.
  Celebrant holds out chalice from centre of altar.
Server pours a few drops of wine into it.
  Celebrant then comes to end of altar to server.
Server pours a few drops of wine into the chalice over the
  Celebrant's fingers, then a little water.
Server pours water on to paten or ciborium if required.
  (The order is easy to remember: wine, wine, water,
  water.)
Server replaces cruets on credence. (He then completes
  the following duties if serving alone.)
If two servers, *A* meanwhile
  Puts out candles
  Opens altar rails

* Even if the Ablutions are taken immediately after the Communion of the People it is pointless to shift the Altar Book to the south end of the altar, which also involves shifting the veil to make room for it. The final prayers and Gloria in Excelsis are said in the centre and the book should remain on the left (see Alcuin Club publications, especially *A Directory of Ceremonial*).

Takes up Altar Book only (as at entrance)
Waits just outside altar rails, leaving centre for priest.
Priest having reassembled sacred vessels joins server(s)
They offer reverence
Server(s) precede(s) priest to sacristy.

VESTRY PRAYER

When they reach the vestry the Priest may say a COL-
LECT and then

Priest: The Lord be with you,
Server: And with thy spirit.
Priest: Let us bless the Lord.
Server: Thanks be to God.

or

Priest: Let us depart in peace,
Server: In the Name of the Lord.
Priest: May the souls of the faithful through the mercy of
God rest in peace.
Server: Amen.

AFTER THE SERVICE

Take off surplice.

IN SANCTUARY

1. Put out candles, if not already done.

2. Replace dust cover (unless there is another Eucharist)
   making sure it is centred, front edge exactly to edge of
   altar but not hanging over in front.

3. Bring back to vestry: Bread Box, Cruets, Lavabo.

4. Replace Alms Dish.

5. Tidy away all books.

1. Always empty water cruet. Refill only if another Eucharist follows.

2. If wine cruet is of metal the wine must be poured back into the bottle. A funnel is needed for this. It should also be poured back if stopper of glass cruet is not airtight.

3. Empty and dry lavabo, putting used towel for washing.

4. Refill Bread Box—especially if there is another Eucharist. But it is always helpful to leave it filled and ready.

5. Cleanse Chalice thoroughly using plenty of water. Dry with clean towel. (There should be one kept specially for this purpose.) Polish off any finger-marks. Rinse purificator and place with lavabo towel for washing.

6. 'Make' chalice and leave ready if another Eucharist follows. Or put away carefully in proper place.

7. Put away Vestments—unless another service follows.

8. Put away Altar Book—unless another service.

OCCASIONAL DUTIES

Many churches have a sacristan who will change altar frontals, perhaps lay out vestments and look after general maintenance. Other churches have no sacristan and the efficient server will keep his eyes open to see what needs doing from time to time, e.g.:

1. RENEWING CANDLES

New candles should always be put in for the great festivals and holy days. Partly burned ones can be used up on ferial Sundays and week days.

When changing candles the foot often has to be pared to fit the candlestick. Spread a newspaper or cloth and *see that no wax escapes*. Make sure candles stand straight.

Both cruets get very dirty inside and the neck is too thin for easy cleaning. Water does not remove the stain.

Scrape up a teaspoon or two of fine ashes or pebbles, the grittier the better, pour them into the cruets, add a little water, shake vigorously. Empty out and rinse and the cruet will be spotlessly clean.

3. STOCK-TAKING

Keep an eye on stocks of Wafer breads, wine, and candles, and report when any of these get low. Make a special point of this a month before great festivals.

SUMMARY OF SERVER'S DUTIES DURING THE SERVICE

Set out in detail the server's work may seem complex. Here is a quick summary for ready reference.

During the actual service the server kneels on the opposite side to the Altar Book. He

1. Leads the **responses** of the congregation throughout.
2. After Epistle transfers **Altar Book** to Gospel side.
3. After the Creed—or Sermon if there is one—at the Offertory **offers** Bread, Wine and water; **receives** alms; **brings** lavabo; **closes** Communion rail.
4. During Communion of the People **stands** at the south side of the altar.
5. After Blessing (or after the Communion of the People) at the Ablutions he
   pours wine, wine, water, water; **opens** altar rails; **may extinguish** candles; may **pick up** Altar Book; goes outside rails and **awaits** Celebrant; **bows** with Celebrant; **leads** Celebrant to Vestry.

The server then gets busy on the after-service duties listed on pages 52, 53.

THE SERVER'S OWN PREPARATION FOR COMMUNION

The aim is to settle quite clearly three things:

What **to confess**; what to give **thanks** for; what to **ask**. When these are decided the Server is ready to receive Holy Communion.

WHAT TO CONFESS. The server at the Eucharist leads the congregation in saying: We acknowledge and confess our manifold sins and wickedness which we from time to time most grievously have committed by thought word and deed. . . . We do earnestly repent and are heartily sorry for these our misdoings. . . .

The server must spend some time on his knees examining his conscience so that these words may mean something and not be just pious nothings. Questions to help his examination of conscience are given on page 57.

WHAT TO GIVE THANKS FOR. Every server has many mercies and blessings to thank God for. The fact that he is a server at all and has the privilege of assisting in the sanctuary is not the least of these. It only needs a few minutes kneeling before our Father in Heaven to settle clearly in our minds the things we most need to give thanks for at that time.

Another name for the Holy Communion is the Eucharist, a Greek word meaning the Great Thanksgiving. We should always give thanks to God because Jesus died on the Cross for us that we might live with our Father in Heaven.

WHAT TO ASK. Try to ask for others' needs as well as for our own. We must not be selfish in our prayers. Always ask that God's perfect will be done, not our own; for our knowledge is very limited. Only God knows what is really best for us. Again, be very definite. You are going to meet the King of kings. Know exactly and clearly what to lay before him. Especially, use the time during the Communion of the People, when you have no serving duties, to bring these three to the throne of grace: your **confession, your thanksgiving, your asking.** This needs concentration and practice but is tremendously rewarding.

To help concentrate and pray, write these three, your confessions, thanksgivings and askings, on a little piece of paper cut to fit into this book. Keep it in the book and use it during the Communion of the People. A place is provided for it on page 47.

QUESTIONS FOR SELF-EXAMINATION

In the Prayer Book it is asked 'What is required of them who come to the Lord's Supper?' The answer given is, 'To examine themselves whether they repent them truly of their former sins . . .'

It is not always easy to remember all the sins we ought to ask God to forgive. There is the good we have failed to do as well as the bad things we remember all too well. To stir up conscience it is important 'to examine ourselves', as the Prayer Book says, by asking questions like these below. Then we know better what we have to own up to and confess.

THE THINGS LEFT UNDONE

Have I tried to serve with reverence?—been thorough?—punctual?—tidy?—dependable?

Have I really tried to learn to pray at the Eucharist?—to master wandering thoughts?—to know Christ's Presence?—

Have I stayed away from church?—kept Sunday holy?—

Have I prepared carefully for Holy Communion?—

Have I read my Bible regularly and carefully?—

Have I missed chances to stand up for my Faith?—have I tried to bring others to church?

Have I given a right share of my money to the Church?—

Have I helped at home as much as I could?—missed chances to do kind acts?—say kind things?

THINGS WE OUGHT NOT TO HAVE DONE

In thought

Have I been jealous?—believed unkind stories about others?—hated others?

Have I been conceited?—spiteful?—unforgiving?

In word

Have I used bad language?—sworn?—used God's name lightly?

Have I lied?—exaggerated?—been deceitful?

Have I told tales about others?—boasted?—told dirty jokes?

In deed

Have I shown off, especially when serving?—failed to get up, when on duty?

Have I done my best at my work?—at school?—at home?

Have I been bad-tempered?—grumbled?—quarrelled?

Have I been greedy?—tried to show off?—taken more than my share?

Have I stolen?—stolen my employer's time?—borrowed and not paid back?

Have I been pure and clean and healthy in all that I do alone?—with others?

Have I been cruel to animals?—neglected a pet?

Have I treated girls with respect and dignity?

Have I degraded sex in thought, word, or deed instead of keeping it holy as God intended?

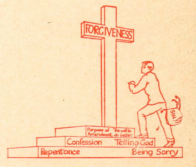

This takes place at the Parish Communion in an interval during the singing of the Gradual, i.e. the hymn after the Epistle.

All the servers should be present and there should be a Corporate Communion of Servers.

Those servers not on duty, robed in cassock and surplice, process in after the choir, led by the processional cross. They are accompanied by the new servers to be admitted, robed in cassock only, who walk first. They occupy places in the choir stalls, or, if there is no room there, places are reserved in the front rows of the nave.

Surplices for those to be admitted are placed, neatly folded, on the altar rails.

Immediately the singing of the Gradual begins the new servers advance two by two to the centre of the altar rails, led by the Head Server who stands at their right (Epistle side).

At the end of the second verse of the Gradual the vicar comes from the altar and faces the new servers, all standing.

Head Server: Reverend Father in God, I present to you .... (Christian name of server) to be admitted as a server at the altar of this church.

Priest: Take care that this candidate be a fit and proper person to be admitted as a server at the altar in the Church of God.

Head Server: I have tried and proved him and believe him so to be.

Priest: My son, what is your desire?

Server: My desire is to serve at the altar.

Priest: Do you promise to be reverent in thought and act in the discharge of all your duties?

Server: I do, God being my helper.

Priest: Do you promise obedience to the Server's Rules and to those in authority over you?

Server: I do so promise.

Priest: Do you promise regularity and punctuality in the discharge of your duties?

Server: I do so promise.

The Server kneels. The Priest places his hand on his head:

Priest: God, who has given you this good will, graciously fulfil the same in you. I admit you, ..., to serve at the altar in this church in the Name of the Father, and of the Son, and of the Holy Ghost; and I clothe you with the white garment of purity—(the Head Server, having taken up the surplice hands it to the vicar, who places it on the server, assisted by the Head Server standing between the server and the congregation).

Priest: See that you so serve God here that you may hereafter be numbered amongst those who, having washed their robes and made them white in the blood of the Lamb, stand before the Throne of God and serve him continually.

All shall say: Amen.

The server kneels. The priest passes to the next. When each has been admitted individually he says:

Bless, O Lord, these thy servants as thou didst bless Samuel who ministered to thy High Priest Eli, and grant them so devoutly to serve at thine altar on earth that they may at the last be counted worthy to worship at thine Altar in Heaven; through Jesus Christ our Lord.

All: Amen.

The Gradual then continues and the servers resume their places. At the Corporate Communion, while the servers in the sanctuary kneel for their Communion, the other servers kneel at the altar rails.

THE
OFFICE
OF
COMPLINE

A late evening
service which
may be used
at a Servers'
Meeting, or
said by a server
privately

THE OFFICE OF COMPLINE

All standing up, the Minister shall say,

The Lord Almighty grant us a quiet night and a perfect end. *Amen.*

Brethren, be sober, be vigilant; because your adversary the devil, as a roaring lion, walketh about, seeking whom he may devour: whom resist, steadfast in the faith.

1 *Peter* **5.** 8, 9.

V.: But thou, O Lord, have mercy upon us;

R.: Thanks be to God.

Minister: O God, make speed to save us;

Answer: O Lord, make haste to help us.

Minister: Glory be to the Father, and to the Son: and to the Holy Ghost;

Answer: As it was in the beginning, is now, and ever shall be: world without end. Amen.

Minister: Praise ye the Lord;

Answer: The Lord's name be praised.

Then shall be said or sung one or more of the following psalms:

PSALM 4. *Cum invocarem.*

1. Hear me when I call, O God of my righteousness: thou hast set me at liberty when I was in trouble; have mercy upon me, and hearken unto my prayer.

2. O ye sons of men, how long will ye blaspheme mine honour: and have such pleasure in vanity, and seek after leasing?

3. Know this also, that the Lord hath chosen to himself the man that is godly: when I call upon the Lord, he will hear me.

4. Stand in awe, and sin not: commune with your own heart, and in your chamber, and be still.

5. Offer the sacrifice of righteousness: and put your trust in the Lord.

6. There be many that say: Who will shew us any good?

7. Lord, lift thou up: the light of thy countenance upon us.

8. Thou hast put gladness in my heart: since the time that their corn, and wine, and oil, increased.

9. I will lay me down in peace, and take my rest: for it is thou, Lord, only, that makest me dwell in safety.

PSALM 31. *In te, Domine, speravi.*

1. In thee, O Lord, have I put my trust: let me never be put to confusion, deliver me in thy righteousness.

2. Bow down thine ear to me: make haste to deliver me.

3. And be thou my strong rock, and house of defence: that thou mayest save me.

4. For thou art my strong rock, and my castle: be thou also my guide, and lead me for thy name's sake.

5. Draw me out of the net, that they have laid privily for me: for thou art my strength.

6. Into thy hands I commend my spirit: for thou hast redeemed me, O Lord, thou God of truth.

PSALM 91. *Qui habitat.*

1. Whoso dwelleth under the defence of the most High: shall abide under the shadow of the Almighty.

2. I will say unto the Lord, Thou art my hope, and my strong hold: my God, in him will I trust.

3. For he shall deliver thee from the snare of the hunter: and from the noisome pestilence.

4. He shall defend thee under his wings, and thou shalt be safe under his feathers: his faithfulness and truth shall be thy shield and buckler.

5. Thou shalt not be afraid for any terror by night: nor for the arrow that flieth by day;

6. For the pestilence that walketh in darkness: nor for the sickness that destroyeth in the noon-day.

7. A thousand shall fall beside thee, and ten thousand at thy right hand: but it shall not come nigh thee.

8. Yea, with thine eyes shalt thou behold: and see the reward of the ungodly.

9. For thou, Lord, art my hope: thou hast set thine house of defence very high.

10. There shall no evil happen unto thee: neither shall any plague come nigh thy dwelling.

11. For he shall give his angels charge over thee: to keep thee in all thy ways.

12. They shall bear thee in their hands: that thou hurt not thy foot against a stone.

13. Thou shalt go upon the lion and adder: the young lion and the dragon shalt thou tread under thy feet.

14. Because he hath set his love upon me, therefore will I deliver him: I will set him up, because he hath known my name.

15. He shall call upon me, and I will hear him: yea, I am with him in trouble: I will deliver him and bring him to honour.

16. With long life will I satisfy him: and shew him my salvation.

PSALM 134. *Ecce nunc.*

1. Behold now, praise the Lord: all ye servants of the Lord;

2. Ye that by night stand in the house of the Lord: even in the courts of the house of our God.

3. Lift up your hands in the sanctuary: and praise the Lord.

4. The Lord that made heaven and earth: give thee blessing out of Sion.

Then shall be read one of the following short Lessons:

Thou, O Lord, art in the midst of us, and we are called by thy name. Leave us not, O Lord our God.   *Jeremiah* **14.** 9.

Or,

Come unto me, all ye that labour and are heavy laden, and I will give you rest. Take my yoke upon you, and learn of me; for I am meek and lowly in heart: and ye shall find rest unto your souls. For my yoke is easy, and my burden is light.

Matthew **11.** 28–30.

Or,

Now the God of peace, that brought again from the dead our Lord Jesus, that great shepherd of the sheep, through the blood of the everlasting covenant, make you perfect in every good work to do his will, working in you that which is well-pleasing in his sight; through Jesus Christ, to whom be glory for ever and ever. Amen.   *Hebrews* **13.** 20, 21.

R: Thanks be to God.

Minister: Into thy hands, O Lord, I commend my spirit;

People: Into thy hands, O Lord, I commend my spirit:

Minister: For thou hast redeemed me, O Lord, thou God of truth;

People: I commend my spirit.

Minister: Glory be to the Father, and to the Son, and to the Holy Ghost:

People: Into thy hands, O Lord, I commend my spirit.

Here may follow this or some other Hymn.

Before the ending of the day,
Creator of the world we pray,
That with thy wonted favour thou
Wouldst be our guard and keeper now.

From all ill dreams defend our eyes,
From nightly fears and fantasies;
Tread under foot our ghostly foe,
That no pollution we may know.

O Father, that we ask be done,
Through Jesus Christ, thine only Son;
Who, with the Holy Ghost and thee,
Doth live and reign eternally.

V.: Keep me as the apple of an eye;
R.: Hide me under the shadow of thy wings.

Anthem. Preserve us, O Lord, while waking, and guard us while sleeping, that awake we may watch with Christ, and asleep we may rest in peace.

Lord, now lettest thou thy servant depart in peace: according to thy word.

For mine eyes have seen: thy salvation,

Which thou hast prepared: before the face of all people;

To be a light to lighten the Gentiles: and to be the glory of thy people Israel.

Glory be to the Father, and to the Son: and to the Holy Ghost;

As it was in the beginning, is now, and ever shall be: world without end. Amen.

Anthem. Preserve us, O Lord, while waking, and guard us while sleeping, that awake we may watch with Christ, and asleep we may rest in peace.

I BELIEVE in God the Father Almighty, Maker of heaven and earth:
And in Jesus Christ his only Son our Lord, Who was conceived by the Holy Ghost, Born of the Virgin Mary, Suffered under Pontius Pilate, Was crucified, dead, and buried, He descended into hell; The third day he rose again from the dead, He ascended into heaven, And sitteth on the right hand of God the Father Almighty; From thence he shall come to judge the quick and the dead.
I believe in the Holy Ghost; The holy Catholick Church; The Communion of Saints; The Forgiveness of sins; The Resurrection of the body; And the Life everlasting. Amen.

Let us pray.

Lord, have mercy upon us.
Christ, have mercy upon us.
Lord, have mercy upon us.

Our Father, which art in heaven, Hallowed be thy name; Thy kingdom come; Thy will be done; In earth as it is in heaven. Give us this day our daily bread. And forgive us our trespasses, As we forgive them that trespass against us. And lead us not into temptation; But deliver us from evil. Amen.

V.: Blessed art thou, Lord God of our fathers;
R.: To be praised and glorified above all for ever.
V.: Let us bless the Father, the Son, and the Holy Ghost;
R.: Let us praise him and magnify him for ever.
V.: Blessed art thou, O Lord, in the firmament of heaven;
R.: To be praised and glorified above all for ever.
V.: The Almighty and most merciful Lord guard us and give us his blessing.
R.: Amen.

We confess to God Almighty, the Father, the Son, and the Holy Ghost, that we have sinned in thought, word, and deed, through our own grievous fault. Wherefore we pray God to have mercy upon us.

Almighty God, have mercy upon us, forgive us all our sins and deliver us from all evil, confirm and strengthen us in all goodness, and bring us to life everlasting; through Jesus Christ our Lord. Amen.

If a Priest be present, he shall pronounce the Absolution:

May the Almighty and merciful Lord grant unto you pardon and remission of all your sins, time for amendment of life, and the grace and comfort of the Holy Spirit. *Amen.*

V.: Wilt thou not turn again and quicken us;
R.: That thy people may rejoice in thee?
V.: O Lord, shew thy mercy upon us;
R.: And grant us thy salvation.
V.: Vouchsafe, O Lord, to keep us this night without sin;
R.: O Lord, have mercy upon us, have mercy upon us.
V.: O Lord, hear our prayer;
R.: And let our cry come unto thee.

Then shall be said one or more of the following Collects:

Let us pray.

O Lord, support us all the day long of this troublous life, until the shades lengthen, and the evening comes, and the busy world is hushed, the fever of life is over, and our work done. Then, Lord, in thy mercy, grant us safe lodging, a holy rest, and peace at the last; through Jesus Christ our Lord. *Amen.*

Visit, we beseech thee, O Lord, this place, and drive from it all the snares of the enemy; let thy holy angels dwell herein to preserve us in peace; and may thy blessing be upon us evermore; through Jesus Christ our Lord. *Amen.*

Lighten our darkness, we beseech thee, O Lord; and by thy great mercy defend us from all perils and dangers of this night; for the love of thy only Son, our Saviour, Jesus Christ. *Amen.*

O Lord Jesus Christ, son of the living God, who at this evening hour didst rest in the sepulchre, and didst thereby sanctify the grave to be a bed of hope to thy people: Make us so to abound in sorrow for our sins, which were the cause of thy passion, that when our bodies lie in the dust, our souls may live with thee; who livest and reignest with the Father and the Holy Ghost, one God, world without end. *Amen.*

Look down, O Lord, from thy heavenly throne, illuminate the darkness of this night with thy celestial brightness, and from the sons of light banish the deeds of darkness; through Jesus Christ our Lord. *Amen.*

Be present, O merciful God, and protect us through the silent hours of this night, so that we who are wearied by the changes and chances of this fleeting world, may repose upon thy eternal changelessness; through Jesus Christ our Lord. *Amen.*

V.: We will lay us down in peace and take our rest;
R.: For it is thou, Lord, only that makest us dwell in safety.
V.: The Lord be with you;
R.: And with thy spirit.
V.: Let us bless the Lord;
R.: Thanks be to God.

The Almighty and merciful Lord, the Father, the Son, and the Holy Ghost, bless and preserve us. *Amen.*

PRAYERS FOR SERVERS

When the Office of Compline is said these prayers for servers may be added. Or they may be used by servers privately.

V.: I will go unto the altar of God,
R.: Even unto the God of my joy and gladness.

O God, who hast entrusted to us the high privilege of serving at the altar, help us become more worthy of this trust. Give us reverence and humility when we serve. Outside the sanctuary keep us loyal to the Faith we hold, staunch in witness, ready in service. May we always live as those who would be with Jesus and would minister with holy things in the courts of Heaven; through him who liveth and reigneth with thee and the Holy Ghost, one God, world without end. *Amen.*

Cleanse us, O God, and keep us undefiled, that we may be numbered among those blessed ones, who having washed their robes and made them white in the Blood of the Lamb, stand before thy throne and serve thee day and night in thy temple; through Jesus Christ thy Son, our Lord. *Amen.*

Servers may repeat together this prayer from the Liturgy of Malabar in India:

Strengthen for service, Lord, the hands
    That Holy things have taken;
Let ears that now have heard thy songs
    To clamour never waken.

Lord, may the tongues which 'Holy' sang
    Keep free from all deceiving;
The eyes which saw thy love be bright,
    Thy blessed hope perceiving.

The feet that tread thy holy courts
    From light do thou not banish;
The bodies by thy body fed
    With thy new life replenish.

TEXTS TO REMEMBER

FAVOURITE PRAYERS